# Mindfulness Meditation

Experience Meditation and Mindfulness and Find Peace Everyday

(Meditations to Reduce Stress, Improve Mental Health and Sleep Better)

**Bobby Leiker**

Published by Rob Miles

© **Bobby Leiker**

All Rights Reserved

*Mindfulness Meditation: Experience Meditation and Mindfulness and Find Peace Everyday (Meditations to Reduce Stress, Improve Mental Health and Sleep Better)*

ISBN 978-1-989990-87-2

All rights reserved. No part of this guide may be reproduced in any form without permission in writing from the publisher except in the case of brief quotations embodied in critical articles or reviews.

## Legal & Disclaimer

The information contained in this book is not designed to replace or take the place of any form of medicine or professional medical advice. The information in this book has been provided for educational and entertainment purposes only.

The information contained in this book has been compiled from sources deemed reliable, and it is accurate to the best of the Author's knowledge; however, the Author cannot guarantee its accuracy and validity and cannot be held liable for any errors or omissions. Changes are periodically made to this book. You must consult your doctor or get professional medical advice before using any of the suggested remedies, techniques, or information in this book.

Upon using the information contained in this book, you agree to hold harmless the Author from and against any damages, costs, and expenses, including any legal fees potentially resulting from the application of any of the information provided by this guide. This disclaimer applies to any damages or injury caused by the use and application, whether directly or indirectly, of any advice or information presented, whether for breach of contract, tort, negligence, personal injury, criminal intent, or under any other cause of action.

You agree to accept all risks of using the information presented inside this book. You need to consult a professional medical practitioner in order to ensure you are both able and healthy enough to participate in this program.

# Table of Contents

INTRODUCTION ................................................................ 1

CHAPTER 1: DEFINING MINDFULNESS .............................. 6

CHAPTER 2: STRESS SYMPTOMS: EFFECTS OF STRESS ON YOUR BODY AND BEHAVIOR .......................................... 23

CHAPTER 3: THE STATE OF FLOW ...................................... 39

CHAPTER 4: HOW TO PRACTICE MINDFULNESS? .............. 53

CHAPTER 5: MINDFULNESS THROUGH BREATH- FIRST STEP TO BEING MINDFUL ............................................................ 70

CHAPTER 6: CALM THE BODY ............................................ 86

CHAPTER 7: HOW TO DO MINDFUL MEDITATION ........... 102

CHAPTER 8: CREATING HAPPINESS .................................. 109

CHAPTER 9: MINDFUL MISTAKES ...................................... 118

CHAPTER 10: WHO AND HOW CAN PRACTICE MINDFULNESS? .............................................................. 128

CHAPTER 11: GETTING READY TO PRACTICE MINDFULNESS ............................................................................................ 142

CHAPTER 12: LEARNING TO BREATHE CORRECTLY ......... 148

CHAPTER 13: IMPORTANCE OF STAYING MOTIVATED ... 155

CHAPTER 14: TECHNIQUES TO CULTIVATE MINDFULNESS ............................................................................................ 165

CHAPTER 15: MINDFUL EXERCISES 45 MINUTES TO AN HOUR ...................................................................................... 171

CHAPTER 16: MINDFUL BODY: CREATING THE BODY YOU WANT WITH NEW CHOICES ............................................. 185

CONCLUSION ...................................................................... 196

## Introduction

Do first, read about it later

At the start of every chapter in this book you'll find a simple 3 minute Mindfulness Meditation exercise. You need to stop reading and DO the exercise. The only way to build a new habit is by doing, which is why the Get The Habit series focuses on taking action right from the start. Do you often buy self-help and how-to books, only to read them from cover-to-cover but never take any action? If this is you, make a commitment right now to DO the 3 minute exercises in this book instead of just reading about them. Do first, read about it later.

3 minutes to success, and why this works

Our brains are hard-wired to conserve energy and be as efficient as possible. Habits are simply the brain's way of saving time – why reinvent the wheel every time you go to complete the most basic task, like getting dressed or making breakfast? But once they are formed, habits – good and bad – are pretty hard to break.

To form a new habit, you have to begin to do things differently, and you have to repeat these actions over and over until they become 'normal' to your brain, and therefore efficient. And the way to do things differently is, well, to just DO IT.

The 3 minutes to success system works so effectively because it's not asking too much of your over-worked brain. Anyone can stop for 3 minutes to practice a new skill. Yes, even you. Anyone can take a 3 minute time-out and begin the process of learning to think and act in different ways. Repeat these 3 minutes often enough and you are building a new habit – in this case a better, healthier habit that will improve your life and dramatically reduce stress.

So why 6 days? Well, it doesn't have to be 6 days. In your case it might take only 5 days of concerted effort, or it might take 7 or 8 days if your brain is a little more resistant to change. But 6 days is the average amount of time it takes to make an impact not only on your mind but also on your daily routine and your family's expectations, and on all those little things you do regularly that right now could be more mindful but aren't.

How to use this book

Do the exercises. Read each chapter. Do the exercises some more. Give yourself the gift of 6 days and 3 minutes at a time – you deserve that, don't you?

You can read a chapter a day, and practice the exercises for that day as often as you can. Or you can read the whole book as quickly as you like, taking time out to practice the exercises when they appear and then making time in your schedule to keep practicing for the whole 6 days. It's up to you! You'll find tips and tricks for mindfulness practice throughout the book, so feel free to dive right in.

Put your skeptical mind aside for a moment, and make a commitment to change. You can live a more mindful life; you can achieve inner calm and increased happiness and a massive reduction in stress. The proof that mindfulness meditation works is out there for anyone to find; the method to make it work for you is right here to discover.

And your journey begins right now ...

## Chapter 1: Defining Mindfulness

Everyone gets that feeling from time to time that the universe is going haywire, and that nothing makes sense anymore. They feel that every action that they do is out of place, and that all plans go wrong.

Even long-term goals that have been made can seem to be impossible to come reach. The result becomes pretty clear – a person may feel the overwhelming stress and pressure when it comes to setting everything right once again.

It would not be too difficult to imagine how stressful an environment can be. People are born to live in a society with clashing beliefs that all claim to have mandate over the other.

There are moments when life does not seem that it can be lived freely, and activities spring out like they are part of a system of forced labor. You may find that you are living in this kind of setting. You may find that you are lacking your center, and you are struggling to find purpose or reason for all things that is happening around you.

Finding Out What is Wrong

Humans are able to think of the different paths that they are going to take, and they are also able to think about them depending on the context that they choose – the past, present, or the future.

However, the way that people think about their choices or they current actions are not always beneficial to them.

There are times when you feel that you could have done more in a certain situation, or that you regret being involved in an act at all. You may also fail to recognize the abundance of opportunities and goodwill in your environment. There are also situations where you are the one who provides that poisonous critique against yourself.

People cannot help but examine every action that takes place around them in the context of the past, and then try to foresee the future using that so-called knowledge. There are many times that you do not want to try something today because you have tried that in the past, and you did not like the results.

However, that may be part of your humanity. People simply try to make quick judgments according to what they have already done, but not according to what could possibly happen NOW.

That is why some beliefs and schools of tradition focus on the idea of channeling one's focus on what is happening now, without paying attention to any other time that may have influenced an event. The idea of focusing in one's current situation is widely known as mindfulness.

The Idea of Mindfulness

Mindfulness, in a nutshell, is giving consideration to the current set of events and to become aware of what is truly happening in an objective way, without judgements. In a sense, it makes someone knowledgeable of the true facts in a situation, as he experiences it.

The idea is this — when you are trying to focus on what is happening around you, you feel that you should observe first, and not be hasty about your decisions or judgment. The result is that you feel that you should suspend thinking too much about the situation according to what you would usually do when you encounter a similar event.

Why People Practice Mindfulness

Refusing to respond hastily to a situation according to old habits would definitely allow you to think more about how to respond the most effectively, instead of mindlessly reacting out of old patterns. Mindfulness has always been one of the most effective tools to slow down and recognize your automatic reactions, and letting you aware of what you should do instead.

By employing mindfulness, you become more aware of the things that you are capable of doing, and not just sticking to your old tricks.

Mindfulness activities also allow a person to slow down and try to understand a situation without going through waves of negative emotions, which would seriously damage one's ability to know what is going on.

By suspending judgment, you become aware that worrying and anxiety is not going to bail you out of a difficult situation, and that you should instead try to keep yourself calm and collected. For that reason, a person who practices mindfulness knows that it would be wise not to act according to illogical stimuli.

The end result is very promising – a person tends to feel a lot more relaxed instead of being pressured to make uncalculated actions that he is fully aware he could not benefit from. He also feels less tension around him – instead of feeling that he is going against the tide, he instead channels his energy to become one with the nature.

Because one is able to suspend one's judgment, he becomes aware that the stress that he usually feels whenever there is a difficult situation actually belongs to the past or the future.

You can easily react from stress trauma, if something similar happened in the past gets triggered in the present. Additionally, you may become prone to worry, if the stress is related to a future event that might arise from what you are doing today. For instance, worrying about paying next month's rent because you had to spend extra money on car repairs this month.

The feeling of fear from a repetition of an untoward event, and the prediction of misery is in fact, an illusion that one creates when he does not decide to live in the present moment. Consider for just a moment how there is no way of truly knowing what the future will hold. Worrying about it will change nothing.

By employing mindfulness, a person makes it a point to see the situation as it is, and that immediately gets him past the idea that he should beat himself up for something that he can never take back, or something that may never even happen.

Because the anxiety you may be feeling towards a situation is alleviated through mindfulness, attention becomes a steering wheel instead of an airbag, you can see the best solution to a problem, and then proceed to action with a much calmer mind.

Creativity and Mindfulness

Only those who are trying to live and act according to what is before them are those who can conveniently climb out of the box that society placed them in. Mindful people are those who does not even think about the certainty of a method – they can invent a strategy right there and then, without being too concerned about so-called time-tested formulas.

Those who live a more mindful lifestyle achieve goals as they should be accomplished, they are also able to do so in an unconventional way.

They do not even have to concern themselves much about rewards form society and will be more willing to welcome criticism from those who think that they know all the rules – they are able to make the own rules of their action by careful observance of what is happening against them.

For these reasons, mindful people easily stand out from the rest of the crowd. They dress according to the weather, not the fashion. They choose work according to the schedule that already works out with their plans, and they are the ones who are spotted as effective problem solvers.

The mindful population does not always act according to the textbook method of doing things – if they spot an error in tradition, it is rather easy for them to debunk it and make their own road.

Components of Mindfulness

Mindfulness is mainly comprised of three components. The first is awareness, which is the state of becoming knowledgeable about one's thoughts and actions. It is also the state of being knowledgeable of how one's body reacts to certain types of stimuli.

The second is being, or being knowledgeable of how the environment moves around you. This is the state wherein you are not tending to act on auto-pilot but instead making actions according to how the entire scene really happens, and not according to the version that you have in your mind.

For instance, instead of automatically laying on your horn when a driver in front of you is still stopped at a green light, you may notice that the person looks old or very upset and will feel more patient. In turn this will leave you feeling much less stressed versus the anger you would normally feel when someone is not doing as you automatically expect them to.

The last component is seeing things and responding according to the knowledge that you have of a specific situation. It means having a specific distance from an event so you can see it how it is really happening, without you in the scene. The knowledge that you gain from achieving different perspectives serves as the rationale for the actions that you will choose.

The Wonders of Mindfulness to Your Health

Mindfulness has been around for a long time — in fact is has been part of eastern philosophies for centuries. The first mention of it is found to be about 5,000 years old, but could be much older than that.

While mindfulness is related to religions such as Buddhism, it does not mean that you need to change your religion if you are planning to practice it. In fact, there had been different branches of scientific studies that aim to teach mindfulness for stress reduction. In that regard, even an atheist can practice mindfulness successfully.

It is no secret that stress can be a cause of physical and mental deterioration. A person who undergoes extreme stress experiences difficulty in sleeping and loss of appetite. After that, chest and neck pains are almost expected. At the same time, extreme stress also increases the risk of a heart attack and blood pressure spikes.

Extreme stress due to worrying and trauma also alters a person's idea of focus, and that can lead to extreme anxiety, depression, and paranoia. Stress can severely alter a person's grasp of reality, and increases the chance of getting a psychological disease such as depression, generalized anxiety disorder or post-traumatic stress syndrome.

Mindfulness-Based Stress Reduction

For the above reasons, psychologists and health practitioners adapted the Mindfulness-based Stress Reduction (MBSR) program in order to help patients cope with heart disease, anxiety, depression, psoriasis, and chronic pain. In fact, this program is the program of choice in the UK to treat recurring depression and is becoming more popular in the United States and the rest of the world.

Since the 1990s, MBSR has been supported by numerous claims that it is indeed an effective program to boost one's physical and mental health. Research found that those who underwent the MBSR program required less visits to a physician, and they are also found to have better antibodies for combating various types of diseases.

Those who also practice mindfulness experience about 70% less anxiety, and they are able to get the best kind of sleep. They are also likely to improve their physical condition while undergoing chronic fatigue syndrome and fibromyalgia. At the same time, they become less prone to certain cancers, diabetes, and heart disease.

Those who consistently practice MBSR are less likely to feel anger, depression, and tension. In other words, those who participated in this kind of treatment are bound to live with a much healthier mind and physique.

## Chapter 2: Stress Symptoms: Effects Of Stress On Your Body And Behavior

Some major symptoms of stress may be affecting your health in more ways than you know. You may believe your persistent throbbing headache, reduced productivity, or insomnia is because of this or that ailment, but in reality, stress could be the major culprit.

Below are common effects of stress:

Common Ways Stress Affects You

Your body, feelings, thoughts, and behavior can be victims of stress. Your ability to recognize the symptoms and signs of stress will give you the ability to manage stress more effectively.

When left unchecked, stress can be the cause of very many health issues such as heart diseases, obesity, diabetes, high blood pressure, etc. Let us learn some common ways stress affects your body, mood, and behavior:

Effects of Stress on Your Body

Headache

Chest pain

Fatigue

Muscle tension and pain

Stomach upset

Sleep disorders

Change in sex drive

Effects of Stress on Your Mood

Anxiety

Lack of motivation or focus

Irritability or anger

Depression or sadness

Feeling overwhelmed

Restlessness

Effects of Stress on Your Behavior

Angry outbursts

Undereating or overeating

Tobacco use

Social withdrawal

Exercising less often

Drug and alcohol abuse

Procrastination and decreased productivity

No matter how much damage stress has caused in your life or how negatively stress affects you, you can still win the war against stress. One great way to live a more stress-free life is to practice mindfulness.

Let us discuss mindfulness techniques you can explore to help you manage your stress levels.

Mindfulness And Meditation: Their Effectiveness Against Stress And How To Practice Them

A number of literatures written support mindfulness and its numerous mental and physical health benefits. Yet, many people who wish to harness the true benefits of mindfulness techniques do not actually understand what mindfulness means and how simple techniques employed during mindfulness exercises can effectively help one achieve such far-reaching and all-encompassing benefits.

Because of this, before we go further, let us take a moment to understand what mindfulness means using an easily understandable approach:

Understanding Mindfulness

We have mentioned mindfulness a number of times. Let us double back a bit and attempt to create an understanding of what it means as well as the different ways you can use mindfulness as a tool in the fight against stress.

In this guide, we will call mindfulness a state of mind, which explains why it can help you live a stress-free life and enjoy your life as you live it moment-to-moment.

By way of conventional definition, we can define mindfulness as your ability to be present, fully aware of where you are and what you are doing, without being overtly reactive or overwhelmed by whatever is happening around you at any time.

We can add to this and say mindfulness is an attribute each of (as human beings) us naturally possesses. When you make it a daily habit and routine, mindfulness can become a readily available part of your life.

Whenever you bring awareness to everything you experience, which you do by bringing complete awareness to your senses, to your state of mind, or to your emotions and thoughts, you are simply being mindful. According to available research studies, training your mind to become mindful is a way of remodeling the physical structure of your brain.

According to Jon Kabat-Zinn, the creator of Mindfulness-Based Stress Reduction (MBSR), the practice of mindfulness lights up parts of your brain not usually activated when you are mindlessly running on autopilot.

The Benefits of Mindfulness

Knowing the benefits of mindfulness meditation will help you understand why it is such a potent tool against stress. Here are scientifically proven ways mindfulness helps you beat stress.

Understand and Gain Control of Your Pain

Pain is something we cannot run away from completely; this we must accept. However, you must never allow pain to rule your life. When you practice mindfulness, you gain mastery over your pain, reshape it, and effectively manage the stress brought on by the pain you experience in life.

Many people suffering from chronic pain now resort to mindfulness for relief. In a recent study conducted at Kaiser

Permanente, Colorado, and that involved 38 participants who suffered from different degrees of back and joint pains, or psychological trauma, using an eight-week Mindfulness-Based Stress Reduction program, researchers assessed the participants before and after the program.

During the class, researchers introduced participants to core MBSR practices that included guided body scan, sitting and walking meditation, and some yoga practices. After taking the course, the participants reported very significant improvement in both physical and mental functions. They also noted a commendable reduction in their use of health services to ease their pain.

Connect Better in your Relationships

Mindfulness keeps you from exhibiting repeated negative behaviors that result from conflicts that might put your relationship in a tailspin. Mindfulness reduces behaviors such as open hostility, being dismissive of your partner, or disengagement.

According to results from a recent study published by the Journal of Social and Personal Relationships, researchers noted that low mindfulness and low self-esteem breed from fear that forces us to cope with the fear in negative ways. However, the study revealed that those with low self-esteem but high mindfulness were less anxious and their behaviors were more stable. Researchers used these results to explain why people who engage in mindfulness exercises experience less stress and exhibit less conflicting behaviors that can weaken the bond between a couple.

Increases Your Ability to Focus

Those who engage in regular mindful practices enjoy better mental focus because mindfulness positively alters brain functions. According to a new study published by the Journal of Neuroscience, mindful people are better equipped to stop the brain activities that cause stress and distractions such as mind wandering.

**According to the study mentioned above and conducted by Italian neuroscientist** Giuseppe Pagnoni, mindfulness exercises such as meditation change brain patterns and increase the participant's cognitive performance. For the study, he recruited 12 Zen meditators who had been consistently meditating for about 3 years. Pagnoni then compared the brain scans o the Zen meditators with those of 12 volunteers of the same age who had never meditated but had the same level of education with the meditators.

His research team put each of these individuals in an MRI machine to measure their brain patterns. The MRI results showed that those who meditated were more stable in their ventral posteromedial cortex (vPMC). The ventral posteromedial cortex is a region in the brain linked to spontaneous thinking and mind wandering—we can find it in the middle of the head on the underside of the brain. The researcher concluded that the vPMC, which is active in most people, plays a very vital role in mental focus.

Having understood the benefits of mindfulness as well as why mindfulness is such a potent tool against stress, let us start discussing how you can practice mindfulness as a way to overcome stress:

The Basics Of Mindfulness Meditation

When adopted as a daily habit, mindfulness helps you put some healthy space between you and your reactions, thereby breaking down your conditioned responses.

Let us discuss how you can tune into mindfulness all through the day as a way of combating stress and living a life of complete freedom from stress.

## Set Some Time Aside For Your Mindfulness Meditation

To sharpen your innate mindfulness skills, you do not necessarily need a meditation bench, cushion, or any special meditation equipment of any kind. Nevertheless, you need to set aside some time and space to engage in daily mindfulness practices.

## Observe the Present Moment Just As It Is

The aim of your mindfulness exercises is not to quiet your mind—though doing so is a secondary part of it. The goal is to pay attention to your present moment without being judgmental of it in any way. In practice, this is usually not as easy as it sounds on paper. However, with due diligence and constant practice, you can pull it off without fail.

Allow Your Judgments to Come and Go

Being judgmental is something that will happen occasionally—even when you are not being intentionally judgmental. To hone your mindfulness, take note of the judgments as they arise during your mindfulness practices and let them pass without dwelling on them for too long.

Always Get Back To Observing the Moment As It Is

Your mind will naturally get lost in a train of thought. Because of this, you need to make mindfulness habitual so that even when your mind wanders, you can return to the present moment repeatedly.

Treat Your Wandering Mind with Kindness

As you practice mindfulness, avoid judging yourself for the thought that comes into your mind and takes your attention away from observing the present moment. When your mind wanders off, which it will do severally, simply recognize it, and then gently refocus on the present moment. Constant refocus on the present moment is the essence, the very heart of mindfulness.

As simple as mindfulness sounds—simple in the way we have described its practice above—its mastery is actually complicated, which mastering mindfulness takes time and practice.

Your task is to keep practicing mindfulness meditation until you can meditate and concentrate on the present moment without your mind drifting off to any other thing, thoughts, place, person, events, etc. Mastery of mindfulness brings with it the level of calmness you need to overcome high stress levels.

Let us see the steps you can take to enjoy the stress-beating effects of mindfulness:

### Chapter 3: The State Of Flow

While talking about mindfulness, it is imperative that we also talk about flow, as the two are often conflated.

Named for the feeling of a water current carrying you along, flow is also known as the zone - a mental state of operation when a person who performs an activity is fully immersed, focused energetically, and is in total involvement with and enjoys the process of the activity. In other words, you are totally absorbed in what you do, and you lose the sense of space and time. This is also known as the "optimal experience."

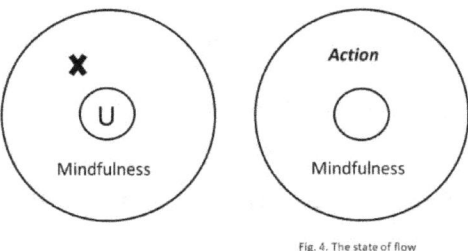

Fig. 4. The state of flow

**Figure 4:** The above-drawn figure shows the difference between flow and mindfulness.

While flow is an aspect of mindfulness, mindfulness and flow are not the one and the same. One of the key aspects of mindfulness is the non-judge mentality of it. With mindfulness, we accept our thoughts, feelings, or bodily sensations as they are. We do not judge them as good or bad. For example, in mindfulness, feeling jealous towards a co-worker who has recently received a promotion is neither good nor bad. It simply is an emotion we are currently feeling.

The flow, on the other hand, is an experience we are completely immersed in. Being in the flow means we have lost all sense of self, space, and even time in lieu of the current event, from which we experience a feeling of immense satisfaction and fulfillment. For example, an author who stays up all night, forgoing sleep and food, to finish a difficult article might achieve a flow state by being thoroughly engrossed in writing the article.

Jeanne Nakamura and Mihály Csíkszentmihályi explain that there are six factors that encompass an experience of flow. While these aspects can all appear independently of each other, only if all six of these appear in combination do they constitute a so-called flow experience?

First of these is to have an intensive and focused mindfulness on the current moment. When achieving flow, the mind must not wander to the happenings of the past hour or day or even the future. Rather, it must stay focused on the present moment. Let's think of a dancer, who enjoys dancing. While in the flow, the dancer does not ponder about the dinner conversation she had the night before with her brother. Rather, she is focused on the dance. All of her efforts and thoughts correlate only to the dance.

The second of these characteristics is to have a feeling of personal rule or agency over an activity or a situation. This isn't to say that one must exert control over every minuscule aspect of the action. Rather, the mind feels at ease with the activity and does not worry about the activity or situation. While in the flow, the dancer does not worry about every single step within the dance. She is not concerned whether she has perfected each of these steps. Rather, she executes the dance to the best of her abilities.

The third of these characteristics is a manipulation of time-related experience. While experiencing a flow, it is common for people to lose track of time. An hour may feel as five minutes or five minutes may feel like 30 minutes. We all know that person who loses track of time doing something they love. The dancer might spend hours dancing a day, only to quickly realize she has forgotten to take a lunch break.

The fourth of these characteristics is the integration of both awareness and action. That is to say the performer and the performance become one, with the performer's full focus being on the performance. While merged together in this way, there is no room in the mind for any other thought including worry, fear, anxiety, etc. The dancer who simply dances, without worry or fear, and becomes one with the dance can thus achieve flow.

The fifth of these characteristics is losing the meditative self-awareness, in which the mind does not need deliberation to do the action necessary to continue the task.

The sixth and last characteristics is that the experience of a task is essentially rewarding. This is also referred to as an autotelic experience. As in the example of the dancer, while she might enjoy finishing the dance and receiving a standing ovation, the dancer simply enjoys dancing itself. It's not the end of the activity that gives the pleasure, but rather the activity itself.[2]

While in a prolonged state of mindfulness, the mind can bring itself into the flow state if all six of the characteristics mentioned above are met.

Like we first discussed at the beginning of the chapter, mindfulness and being in the flow - while connected - are not the same. There is a multitude of differences between the two.[3]

Mindfulness is intentionally tuning into yourself to achieve full awareness of the present moment. While in a flow, you break through a barrier where you find yourself experiencing immense happiness, confidence, and freedom.

Another key difference is the relationship between mindfulness and the flow state. The key relationship in the flow is between the performer and the performance. To get into the flow, we consistently redirect our attention to a task. The relationship that is highlighted in mindfulness is with one's own mind. To achieve mindfulness, we redirect our attention inward to ourselves.

Meditation is usually the key to mindfulness; whereas a wide number of activities can be utilized to achieve a flow state. Only the person's individual relationship to the activity matters. For example, a dancer can achieve a situation of flow through dance, while an author can achieve through writing.

Mindfulness can be taught by specialized trainers. In fact, many people attend meditation classes to achieve mindfulness. However, the flow cannot be attained through specialized training. Rather, it must be achieved through one's unique relationship with an activity.

There are three important factors in mindfulness: **pause, breathe** and **notice**. To achieve mindfulness, we must first push ourselves to pause many activities. The next step is to take deep breaths that will slow us down. This will lead us to notice the environment around us, causing a heightened awareness.

The following exercises call upon these three factors to help you achieve mindfulness.

Mindfulness Exercise # 2: Breathing

We breathe and that is why we are here. At the core of the human life, we cannot survive without our ability to draw in each breath and let it out. Yet, it is an action that we ignore for a good portion of our daily lives.

Set aside five minutes of "my time" as you are waiting for the bus or the train or simply take a five-minute break during your hectic work schedule every day to practice mindfulness through breathing.

Start by closing your eyes and slowly breathing in through your nose and letting it all out. Make sure you pay close attention to your abdomen inflating and flattening with each breath. Breathe in and out slowly until you find yourself in a rhythm.

This breathing exercise calms your mind and slows down your pace. It forces you to intentionally put a pause in your day to focus your attention on one simple thing - your breath. This allows you to breathe smoothly, resulting in your brain receiving more oxygen, which clears your thinking. Your action is now in-sync with your intention.

Mindfulness Exercise #3: Grounding

This exercise can be done in conjunction with the breathing exercise above. Find the rhythm in your breathing and continue to focus on that for a few breaths.

Once you're comfortable in the rhythm, refocus your attention on your feet. Feel your feet touching the ground. If you are wearing shoes, you can also feel the sole of your shoe touching the ground.

This exercise connects you to the Earth. It makes you feel your presence at the moment.

You can do this exercise while walking or sitting down. The purpose of this exercise is to let your mind know that you are in control of your body.

This is a good exercise to do especially while feeling frustrated or stressed out. It is always good to remind yourself that you are in control of your emotions, instead of letting the emotions control you.

You can use this exercise to ground yourself instead of letting the negative emotion lifting you off the ground.

## Chapter 4: How To Practice Mindfulness?

There are several techniques that you can do to practice mindfulness. We will not of course dwell on the psychotherapy part, but rather focus on the things that you can do in your everyday life, minus the need for a professional help.

Simple Ways to Integrate Mindfulness in Your Daily Life

Pay careful attention or an act of "mindful listening" - If you're a beginner, you start with mindful listening. This is a perfect because on a daily basis, we encounter different people and most of the time, conversations will just pass by (unless particularly interesting for you). As someone talks to you (even people whom you have close attachments), the usual scenario is that you are physically present, but your mind is actually wandering. You might give some indications that you are listening, but in reality, you are just hear the words. There will also be times that you are listening, but at the same time you are mentally judging these people you're talking to, criticizing them, agreeing or disagreeing with them, even before they were able to finish their stories. In short, we are caught up with our own mental chatter, and chances are you have missed a lot of important details, subtle hints and more in the conversation.

To practice mindfulness, you have to REALLY listen to what they are saying, and what they are not saying. Give them all your attention. Stop what you are doing, listen and turn-off the inner comments and judgments that you may have. Your aim here is to develop the habit of listening and understanding people and stripping your mind of the usual negative judgment that we all give to other people.

The effect? Not only will you not miss out the details of the things that they are saying (especially the non-verbal cues) but the next time that you will also speak to them, they will also give you the same courtesy of listening to you intently. This will create a connection between the two of you. Plus you will begin to appreciate the uniqueness of others, and they will see the goodness in you. This is a simple act of love that we can give to others.

Transform housework chores - who would have thought that your usual household chores can be a road to mindfulness? You may not realize it, but our household chores actually takes a portion of your time. Do not let that precious time pass you by or rush into things dreading the chores.

Change your mindset, be engaged in what you are doing, eliminate mindless chatters that you have and make every task some sort of a ritual. Be in tune with the moment.

For example, you have to do the dishes, you actually "hate" the idea and as usual, will rush into finishing it. But why not view it in a different way? Be aware of the running water, feel the movement of your hands, make it a "quiet" time. Be in sync with the task. Do not waste your time hating what you do, instead embrace it. If you stayed in that state, chances are, your tasks are not properly done, a plate might slip, which will result to more tasks since you have to clean it up. You are also extinguishing the joy that you might have felt for the day.

Familiarize yourself with the old stuff - why not take the time to roam around the house, pick something that has been there for ages. Look at these items with a different set of eyes. You will be pleasantly surprised to find new details that you have not noticed before. The new found awareness will bring you closer and fonder to the things and people around you.

Eating mindfully - this is one thing that most people don't do. Take pleasure in eating, in fact, this is one avenue in life that you can derive pleasure on. When eating, make it as an experience (chefs and foodies actually do this). First look at the presentation, take notice of the scent, and as you start eating, make sure to take small bites and chew slowly. Savor the taste and even the texture of the food. As you do this, you will begin to actually taste different flavors, the food may seem to taste yummier as you used all of your senses.

In effect, not only will the food taste better, but you are actually preventing yourself from overeating so it also helps promote proper digestion.

Observe your thoughts - through careful watching of the mind; you are actually letting mindfulness in your system. Do just be swept away by your stream of thoughts. Keep in mind that not all thought patterns are actually true and correct, especially with anxiety-related thoughts. Chances are, these thoughts are not the reality, but can even be just a figment of your imagination that spurted from the things that you are dreading. When you become mindful, you will realize that these thoughts should not have any hold on you. You do not have to act it out. You will begin to recognize where it stemmed out. When you take a pause, you will have a clear sense of your next step. So the next time that you will observe the same thought pattern again, you can swat it out before it can create havoc with your thoughts and emotions.

Say no to multi-tasking – you might raise an eyebrow on me, especially since we live a very busy world. But if you actually want to be productive, then you have to break this habit. Give all your attention to the one task that you are doing, clear your mind of the other noises. You will be surprised as ideas seem to flow better, rooms for creativity becomes bigger, and you are actually consuming less time to complete your tasks.

According to studies, if you multi-task or switch from one task to another, you actually lose 40% of your productivity!

Embrace each task given, take one task at a time and discover more things about yourself and that particular task at the assigned time.

Try mindful walking - this is another everyday task that you can integrate with mindfulness. When you walk, don't just walk with the destination in mind. Walk with the purpose of being mindful. What do I mean? Before even taking a step, feel your muscle moving as you go into a standing stance, pay attention to your body, the feeling of your feet as they hit the ground, observe your surroundings, don't rush, just be present, enjoy the moment and feel everything. Walking will be an act of meditative exercise

Handle negative emotions and stress through mindfulness - stress and negative emotions (anger, sadness, guilt and more) are actually a normal part of life. There are a number of triggers for this like an angry boss, financial problems, relationship problems and more. We all have different responses to this, some may retaliate, some may fall into depression, and some may even have physical manifestations like palpitations and more. As discussed, mindfulness is helpful on this situation. So how can you handle the negativity? "Detach yourself" by observing your thoughts and emotions, you can give labels to these thoughts, you can feel the emotions or choose some techniques to calm you down, like breathing exercises. After having that labeling-observing process, or as you acknowledge the emotions and clearly pinpoint the reasons, you can now mindfully choose the next course of your action. Escaping is not an option in mindfulness, rather, you have to live the moment.

Practical tips:

1. Choose to start your day rather than letting the day start you - begin each day by noticing the sensations of the breath for a few seconds before jumping out of bed.

2. Use transitions wisely - choose some days to drive to and from work without

the radio or phone. When you arrive at your destination, allow yourself a few seconds to sit in the car, noticing the breath.

3. Nourish yourself - mindfully eat your lunch attending to the colors, taste, and smells of the food.

4. Just walk between meetings - no emails or texts, feeling the feet on the floor, the air on the skin, and the possibility of greeting colleagues you pass rather than bumping into them while you text!

5. Sit at your desk - while your computer is turning on, noticing the sensations in the body as you sit.

Try one each day, what did you notice? What other Purposeful Pauses do you discover?

Bonus: Breathing exercises.

Again, there are different ways on how you can employ mindful meditation, but I will teach you the easiest and "simplest" way that you can do to practice mindful meditation. You can set aside a specific time per day, this could also act as your quiet time. This involves there simple steps:

Choose a quiet spot wherein distractions are less likely to occur; it might be at the corner of your bedroom, or in your garden.

Just sit on your chosen spot, do not slouch (if you are comfortable lying down, you may also do so), just feel the moment, focus on your breathing, pay attention to the air that is coming in and out your nostrils. Just examine the sensations, feeling and even the mental state neutrally (note it).

You are not trying to have a "blank" mind, but when you stop noticing your breathing, forgot that you are sitting, and your mind is just wandering ( this is normal especially if you are fairly new to meditation), just "gently" pull your mind back to your breathing. Again, just feel the moment. Let the calmness wash over you.

Remember that in this type of meditation, your goal is not to change your ways, but to actually become aware of what is really true at that specific moment. Your goal is to be present regardless of what is happening. You are training your mind to be unconditionally present, be free from distractions and have an improved focus. For beginners, you can try this for 10-15 minutes.

This exercise is very simple, it will take not much time, requires no equipment and can be done everywhere. Although you can do this exercise in any position, sit with your back straight while learning the exercise. Place the tip of your tongue just behind your upper front teeth, and keep it there through the entire exercise. You will be exhaling through your mouth.

Try pursing your lips slightly if this seems difficult.

Exhale completely through your mouth, making a whoosh sound.

Close your mouth and inhale quietly through your nose to a mental count of 4.

Hold your breath for a count of 7.

Exhale completely through your mouth, making a whoosh sound to a count of 8.

This is one breath. Now inhale again and repeat the cycle three more times for a total of four breaths.

Sit in a comfortable position with the spine straight and head slightly forward. Gently close your eyes and take a few deep breaths. Then let the breath come naturally without trying to influence it.

Ideally it will be quiet and slow, but depth and rhythm may be different.

To begin the exercise, count "1" to yourself as you exhale.

The next time you exhale, count "2," and so on up to "5."

Then begin a new cycle, counting "1" on the next exhalation.

Never count higher than "5," and count only when you exhale. You will know your attention has wandered when you find yourself up to "8," "12," even "19."

Try to do 15 minutes of this form of meditation.

## Chapter 5: Mindfulness Through Breath- First Step To Being Mindful.

Breathing as mindfulness practices are very helpful because; if you can control your breathing, you can start controlling the way you react to situations around you. The mindfulness practice of breathing means; to observe and be mindful of your breathing patterns.

It means you choose a breathing cycle and then pay attention to it as fully as you can. You may want to vary the time it takes for a breath as it moves through your nostrils, likewise, you can vary the contraction / expansion of the abdomen and chest while you perform the breathing exercises. Keep in mind that the objective here is to observe your everyday sensation. At the beginning of the breathing exercise, you may be distracted, for instance by the sounds emanating nearby (sounds of television, or people), hence you should consider choosing a quiet place to perform your mindful breathing exercises.

You need to be aware of your breathing when performing these exercises, that is why you should try and maintain focus and prevent any thought from interfering with your breathing cycles. If a thought forces itself into this exercise, you must guide the attention back to the breathing activities.

Just like in other forms of mindfulness exercises, the first part is to be aware of the present circumstances or present moment, and the second part is to accept that your mind will wander from the moment occasionally and there is no need to judge the thoughts even if it is a "negative one"- the objective is to guide your thoughts back to the exercise you are performing.

One thing you will notice if your mindful breathing exercises are effective is that the number of distracting thoughts will reduce gradually as you repeat the breathing exercises, because you are now being empowered to focus on the moment.

You may be asking yourself the question; what is so special about mindful breathing exercise? The answer is simple- it helps you focus on one thing at a time and not several thoughts trying to distract you.

Breathing exercises can be an indication of our stress level- if you find it difficult to focus on one thing (such as the air blasting your face or a bird flying in the sky), it means your stress level is high and you may not be able to maintain direct focus.

The good thing about the mindful breathing exercises is that you can observe it at any time of the day, whether you are in the supermarket, even in the traffic or work place. One thing you should learn is that, as you let the thoughts go, you will be able to let distracting thoughts go. The ability to let go off your breath also means you are learning to let an emotion run its course without holding on to it. Mindful breathing exercises are very helpful for those suffering from depression, caused by repetition of certain thoughts and emotions on daily basis.

Simple steps to mindful breathing

Step #1: Take an erect and comfortable posture and close your eyes gently.

Step #2: bring your focus and attention to the floor you stand or sit on and for a few minutes, explore the sensations at the contact between your body and the floor.

Step #3: Bring your mind or awareness to the fluctuating patterns of sensations between your body and the floor surface (for instance, is it getting warmer or colder?), and breathe in and out.

Step #4: Shift your focus from the floor and place a hand on your abdomen as you breath in and out – feel the physical sensations emanating from your abdominal walls. As each breathe stretches your abdomen, make sure you pay careful attention and adjust the speed of your breathing occasionally. At this stage, your mind is totally aware of your breathing pattern and not the physical sensations between your body and the floor.

You may want to shift attention away from your breathing pattern, back to the sensations between your body and the floor, just make sure you ignore the thoughts of the stretching of your abdomen.

Advance mindful breathing exercises

#1: The Rhythmic breathing for concentration

While you settle for this breathing exercise, you need to perform the following steps

Step #1: Relax yourself into a full and relaxed rhythmic breathing just before you start your breathing practices. Keep in mind that the quality of your breathing will depend on the quality of your preparedness and practice steps.

Step #2: As a beginner, your breathing may still be controlled by the tension remaining in your body, and your initial regular patterns, but don't worry, you will get over such obstacles. Make sure you attain a state where your breathing comes in and out smoothly (you can maintain a rhythmic patter of 2-3 seconds breathe in and 2-3 seconds breathe out.

Step #3: Do not force this procedure, if you do, you will create another form of tensed state, hence you may end up distracting yourself from the exercise.

Step #4: Repeat this exercise until you are able to maintain a steady time space between breathing in and out without losing concentration.

#2 Breath stretching

You need to learn to stretch your breath during mindful breathing practices, and the reason being that it will help you relax even more, and you will be able to commit yourself even more to other mindful activities.

Step #1: To start your breathing stretching exercise, simply start by inhaling and count slowly, numbers 1-6, hold your breath at 3 and then exhale at 6, then hold at 2 before exhaling at 4. Repeat this step.

Step #2: If you feel you are short of breath, simply let the breathing pattern go until you become comfortable, and then return to breath-holding step above.

Step #3: As the breath-holding become easier, you can increase it to a count of 8, 10 and so on, and make sure you hold on the half the counts (for instance, hold at 4, 5 and so on).

Step #4: once you have worked your breathe for about 10 minutes, you can then relax into your normal breathing ways.

#3: Mind settling exercises

Getting your mind settled through breathing techniques, is one of the most important steps you must take if you want to live in the present moment. One of the main principles of mindful breathing is that if your focus remains scattered then your energy will be scattered.

Settling the mind will not only help you achieve new skills, it will also help you bring your blood pressure and stress levels under control, thus prolonging your life.

Step #1: Do not try to force your mind to be silent, you will end up adding more pressure and create tension. Instead you should watch out for silence underneath the noises generated by the daily random thoughts.

Step #2: Pay more attention to your breathing rate.

Step #3: As new thought begins to come up, focus more on your breathing patterns, no matter how prevalent such thoughts are. As you gradually return your focus to your breathe, you will gain more control of your mind, and this will force your mind to become quieter.

#4: Body relaxation

Body relaxation techniques are key to healthier body, likewise they help you develop better skills in handling other mindful techniques. Body relaxation is part of mindful mental practices; however, you can practice them along with your breathing exercises.

Step #1: Examine yourself from head to toe and release tension gently as you do so.

Step #2: Repeat the first step three times.

Step #3: Make sure each and every part of your body feel at ease and heavy and never stay rigid and tensed up. Make sure all muscle anxiety dissipates gradually as you repeat the steps, and let your body feel like you are sinking into the ground.

Just like any other practice in Mindfulness, breathing techniques must be practiced on daily basis, until you incorporate the idea into your daily lifestyle. When you take a deep breath before you react to an unpleasant situation, there are possibilities that you will make a more rational cecision that wouldn't hurt your feelings later on.

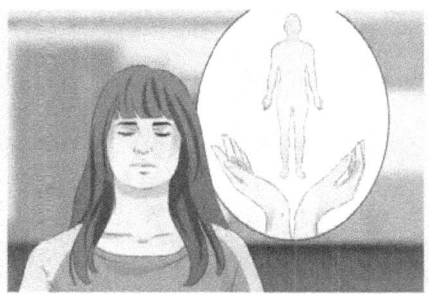

#5: Create a unison between your breathing and movements

Qigong is best achieved when there is unison between your movements and breathing patterns. Unless you are otherwise instructed for certain movements, you must ensure that you maintain a deep, relaxed and eve breathing patterns. Since movements and breathe are linked, you must take the movements slow while you maintain the deeply-rooted relaxation.

In summary, mindful breathing exercises will help you observe some sensations that are connected to your breathing patterns. For instance, the rise and collapse of your abdomen while you inhale and exhale will help you prevent distractions and get immersed in the moment.

When you use equal breathing timing, you will be able to calm your mind even when there are racing thoughts getting out of control in your mind. Mindful breathing can also be very helpful when it becomes difficult to get some sleep.

## Chapter 6: Calm The Body

Pressure is a normal brain reaction. This keeps us out of the way of damage when our stress system works well. It alerts us to changes in our surroundings and gives us time for hazard evaluation and comfort adjustment. This starts with our senses; our eyes, ears, nose and skin are always searching for changes in our surroundings. The information they obtain is sent to the information interpreting hypothalamus (in our brain). This indicates the function of the pituitary and adrenal glands when danger is detected. Together they release hormones that increase blood pressure and heart rate, including cortisol and epinephrine, into the blood. We also provide our body with more strength so that we can fight or run away. In countless situations, this stress response is extremely helpful. It's hurrying us to stay on schedule or get out of a major speeding truck's way. When the temperature is high, it signals us to take off a sweater and take shelter when there is a storm. Nonetheless, with an intervention, this stress response is meant to be resolved. The body systems are designed to cycle with rest or restorative times in between by stress-resolution cycles.

If tension goes untreated, it results in unnecessary demands on our body for prolonged periods. Ultimately, stress can compromise many of our body's systems, resulting in gastrointestinal problems, increased risk of heart disease, autoimmune system depression, and memory impairment. The elevated levels of cortisol and epinephrine often induce a heightened shock reaction, so worrying someone who is already overwhelmed does not take long-becoming a vicious cycle.

Anxiety is more of an emotional response that is connected to it with a sense of concern or fear. A thinking or feeling that we are "not free" usually drives the concern. It's not a warning that our ears, nose, or eyes are telling. Memories, beliefs or expectations remind it. It is not always understood the root of fear or concern. But as our brain is mulling over these thoughts, it will often trigger a response to stress— by alerting our body to "risk" that may not exist in reality. In effect, the body reacts in preparation for fighting or running with that high-stress response. This is a physical response to an emotional situation and an indication of the relation between the mind and the body.

The connection between mind and body is when the body reacts to something that the mind thinks. An example would be, you can raise your heart rate if you think of a very stressful situation in your life. By contrast, you can lower your heart rate if you think of a stress-free, calm and pleasant time; all without moving from your chair. You can also experience this connection with sounds, smells and pictures that remind you of happy/good or challenging/bad things.

Without awareness, our health and emotional well-being can be challenged by both stress and anxiety. Both can compete with the way we live the life we want to lead and have better relationships for us. They can cost us time, money and connections if they are unattended; ultimately our health and well-being. Think about what stress and anxiety have cost you so far; healthy digestion, peaceful sleep, a body free from pain, a job, relationship, advanced degree? Fortunately, they can be identified, controlled, managed or eliminated with education and focused attention.

Body Tricks to Calm Your Anxiety

Brain is often called the body's boss, but it is also true that the body can have an enormous influence on the brain. It is possible to relieve your anxiety and reduce its impact on your health and happiness by using the natural abilities of your body.

By using these' tricks' of your body whenever you feel anxiety, you can help you regain your balance and get on with your life.

Rocking psychologists don't know why this works for certain, nor does anyone seem to agree on a theory. All they know is it's working. After numerous tests with patients with anxiety, they came to that conclusion but it is something parents intuitively know. You calm the body and the mind by rocking gently-you may often notice that people do this when they grieve or are highly emotional. It's a nervous laugh-like reflexive action-used by the body to mask and reduce anxious feelings. You can turn this around and use it when anxiety strikes to help calm your nerves.

Feet Up: This may not be practical in the company, but it's a great way to release the pent-up stress and tension of an anxiety attack when you're alone. Only lie on the floor on your back and put your feet on a chair, couch or other elevated platform. To support the spine, place a soft towel under your neck. Not only because you are in a state of rest, this position has a deep psychological effect, but it also has many physiological benefits.

Next, it helps restore the spine and neck to their proper place-releasing muscle stress and tension. Second, it slows the heart to a more steady rhythm that helps with your overall anxiety condition.

The Unfolding Spine Your body begins to tighten up your spine, shoulders and neck as you feel tense from anxiety. Operating through the body, stress and anxiety influence your posture and alignment. The Unfolding Spine Exercise is a simple exercise intended to relieve the stress in your spine and thus help you return to a state of equilibrium-to cure your anxiety. Only stand up and try to relax while dropping your upper body to the floor gradually-keeping your legs straight. As if touching your toes is reaching you. As you do this, you slowly breathe out and feel your back and neck muscles give way to gravity when you fold forward. When you reach down as far as you can wait a second as you take a deep and refreshing breath before you slowly start to rise again. Feel rejuvenated as you return to your balanced state. Do this a couple of times or as long as you feel anxious to restore calm.

Best Ways to Calm Your Body and Mind

When you follow these simple tips to calm your body and mind, you're on the best way to find relief from stress and anxiety, better cope with everyday problems, be stronger emotionally and boost your focus. You can get better, more tolerant and more out of life. Generally speaking, the most effective way to overcome stress and anxiety is not so much to try to change the situations, but simply to change the way you deal with them.

There are many ways to calm body and mind, from physical (massage, acupressure, etc.) to mental (influencing the subconscious) and metaphysical (tapping the inner spirit into the universal life force). I'll give you a few starters in this section so that you can start to relax instantly. Training is always more!

Improve your fitness-a fit body can cope with stress much more, and there is a lot of satisfaction to gain from physical fitness and achievement. Start slowly and don't overdo it, but develop your strength steadily.

Change your eating habits you do what you're eating-try eating more vegetables and less fat and see how easily your body will react and change your ability to relax.

Upgrade your drinking habits-take a glass of water or herbal tea instead of coffee. When you feel anxious, try to reduce the body's tension on stimuli such as caffeine or alcohol.

Enhance your posture: your shoulders slumped and your neck lowered hinder proper breathing. Simplify and feel like it feels good to stand up to you.

Get comfortable: Remove your shoes to calm down and relax, undo your tie or neck button, loosen your belt, unclutched your bra, slip into something comfortable.

This is the requirement for any practice of relaxation.

Fresh air: breathe in the fresh air and open the windows.

Slow down: It takes a few minutes outside to slow down instead of talking and looking for a business at any cost. Nature has a way to calm your mind.

Silence: find a place in silence-treasure it, absorb it, plunge into it, and hang on to it for as long as possible. With a place of quiet, several calming exercises will begin.

Track your breathing: straighten up and take a deep slow breath through your nose, down into your tummy, don't let your chest rise, relax your back, and slowly release your breath through your mouth.

Muscle relaxation: the muscles of one arm contract easily to sit or lie-hold it-then let them go slack and feel the difference. Save the feeling of comfort. Do the same with the other arm and legs one at a time Shoulders and neck: slowly rotate back and forth one side, then up and down. Do the same thing with the other shoulder. Let your head fall softly on your arms, then bring it back and up. Tilt your head to the left and right shoulder after that. Slowly repeat this.

Jaw release: open and close your mouth wide. Repeat that a couple of times. Then put your fist under your nose, open your mouth, and push against your fist the lower jaw. Keep on for a couple of seconds, then release.

Hands: hold the fingers firmly, then release. Be mindful of the sensation of distress. Then nestle your left in your right hand, brushing each other's thumbs softly. Stay this way and relax.

Motivation: motivate yourself to stay calm on your path. Seek it actively; if you are certain that you can do it, you will be propelled forward by positive energy.

Reject stress: reorganize your goals distinctly. Reject anything that puts you under pressure. Learn to say no and become more energetic and positive.

Comment: This is a wide range of possibilities. Try to imagine a certain situation (for example, you can cope with a stressful situation), then imprint it on a stone or small item that you can fit into your pocket. Then you will see this picture every time you touch it and believe that you can do it.

Autogenic training: This is also a big field and a good way to respond to emergency stress. Lie down, think about your weapons. Feel heavy on them. Think again and again: "My arm gets heavy." Do the same with each leg and the other neck. You can also think and repeat: "My arm gets wet." Feel the warmth of it.

Influence your subconscious: there is no way like this to reinforce messages to your subconscious, such as "I'm calm and can cope with this situation."

Visualization: go to sleep in your mind with a vision of how you want to be. Repeat this over and over, every night. Try to wake up in your mind with this image.

Concentrate on the task at hand: if you are immersed in a task in order to achieve the best outcome you can achieve (this can be anything at all, such as washing the dishes, ironing, driving a car or mowing the lawn), you will find that task becomes like a meditation in itself. You derive satisfaction from your efforts, time flies, and you spend at least this time solely here and now, not thinking about the past or future.

## Chapter 7: How To Do Mindful Meditation

Mindful meditation is a great foundation in helping to form or develop insight, as well as improving your skills in meditation practice. You can use this form of meditation everywhere as it helps you to explore all aspects of your mind and body. Mindful meditation has many hidden benefits such as posing as an anchor to help your mind from becoming lost in feelings and thoughts, helping you to develop skills that will improve the quality of your life. It will help you to learn how to develop deeper concentration skills, helping you to focus on the task at hand.

Choosing a Place to Meditate. An ideal location for you to meditate would be one that is not too light or dark, or too hot or too cold. Avoid places that are going to be filled with distractions, and disturbances. If it feels comfortable you can do it outside. If you tried to practice in one place, but it didn't feel right somehow then look for another spot that seems like the right fit for you. You don't have to go to a meditation centre, only if you prefer to do your meditating in a group. You can find a quiet room in your house, perhaps your bedroom to do your meditation in.

Deciding on a Suitable Posture. You need to find a posture that best suits you—it may be standing, walking, sitting, or lying down. Each of these postures has their advantages and disadvantages. It is advised that you try each posture one at a time until you have a good sense of what is going on, and have become more practiced and aware. Don't try and do them all at once this could end up causing you frustration and causing you not to want to continue. It is best to trial one at a time, after having some practice and experience with each.

Standing Posture. The standing posture is the upright posture. Your hands must be raised with your palms facing you at a comfortable angle and height. Find a position that your arms feel comfortable, having minimal tension or effort. You can also put them at your side.

- Relax your stomach and lower back

- Your feet should be shoulder width apart with your weight evenly dispersed between them, your knees should not be locked

Reclining Posture.  The reclining posture is also referred to as the lion posture.  It involves you lying on your right hand side, resting your head on your hand, or a small pillow.  Your left hand rests on top of your body.

- If you find that this posture is affecting your circulation then try a different posture

Lying on Back.  Lying on back is a common posture for many beginners.  Just make sure that it doesn't cause you to fall asleep.

Seated Posture. The seated posture of meditating has a variety of different styles, find the one that suits you and that you are most comfortable with. Some of the different variations have the legs crossed, both legs folded with feet facing up is known as the "full lotus," when legs are folded one on the other this is known as the "half lotus." The important thing is you find a position that you feel most comfortable doing, make the choice to suit you not the position that your friend may prefer.

• You can have your hands lightly resting on the top of your legs with palms facing up, or palm facing down.

- You may have your hands folded in you lap, or just resting on your thighs and knees.

- Your neck should be balanced and your head should be slightly tilted back to open airways.

- Your chest should be upright and open and your lower back and stomach should be relaxed.

Walking Posture. The walking posture is found to be the best posture for many practicing mindfulness meditation. It gives a lot while having very few disadvantages. This posture allows you to incorporate your mindfulness into your day-to-day experiences. Walk at a slow gentle pace, this is usually done over a small distance going forwards and backwards. It is best to do it in an area that is secluded with no distractions. When walking you are doing what is called empty stepping in that when you move your foot you redistribute or shift your weight after it has been placed.

• Your hands can be clasped or hang gently by your side

• You can focus on different parts of your body such as your feet, legs, chest, and hips as well as the intention to move.

## Chapter 8: Creating Happiness

The impact of mindfulness on our happiness cannot be gainsaid. If we are happy, we enjoy our lives and become optimistic as we face the future. Mindfulness bestows this wondrous feeling of happiness in various ways.

Strengthens relationships

Our life partners play an important role in our lives. If you settle down with the right person, your life will become great, but if you settle down with the wrong person, everything will go to the dogs. But what is never highlighted is the fact that strong relationships take work. The partners must each play their roles in order for the relationship to work. Practicing mindfulness not only allows one to play their role well but also makes them the best version of themselves. The following are some of the ways that mindfulness improves a relationship.

Attentiveness: Modern life can be hectic, but sadly most people know not to separate their work life from family life. You will found spouses paying attention to everything else under the sun but one another. Their time is drained away in things like endless updating of their social media, watching movies, reading emails, and completing their work assignments. But mindfulness helps partners to have a strong relationship going by encouraging them to pay attention to one another and spend a lot of time together.

Lowers negative emotional reaction: You and your partner certainly have different life experiences, goals, and values. The things that disgust you may not apply to your partner. And this is a perfect recipe for conflict. You're likely going to find fault with the things that they do and vice versa. But now what? Should you allow minor inconveniences sabotage what is otherwise a great relationship? By no means! You should both learn to have acceptable emotional reactions. Mindfulness helps a person lower their negative emotional reaction, thus making them less hostile and more fun to be around, an attitude that gives way to an amicable resolution of conflict.

Promotes collaboration: At the end of the day, the success of a relationship relies on the collaborative efforts from both partners. When one partner shoulders most of the burden of the relationship, problems will arise. Through mindfulness, partners become more adept at working as a team and this not only lightens their burden but also brings them closer to one another.

Promotes empathy

Can we become happier by trying to put ourselves in other people's shoes? Yes! Showing others empathy affects the judgments that we end up making. For instance, if one of your trusted employees fails to meet the goals that you had set for them, you can be easily frustrated. But if you learn about the challenges that made it impossible to achieve their goals, you may empathize and it won't hurt as much. Actually, it won't hurt at all. The more empathy you show toward people, the more connections you will have and ultimately you stand to benefit from the kindness of other people as well. But if you're a ruthless person, everyone will run away from you and during your challenging times, you will have no one to run to. Our happiness in a great way relies on the connections that we have and in order to enjoy the company of other people, we have to have a certain level of empathy.

Promotes laughter

A world devoid of laughter is a terrible world. But that is the reality of most people across the world. We are staggering under the weight of challenges and bad experiences. And this has taken away our capacity to recognize and appreciate any humor. But when we calm down our raging thoughts, when we get rid of our anxieties and start looking at life through the lens of objectivity, we are open to having fun and sharing laughter again. Studies have shown that having a sense of humor not only increases our happiness but also boosts our capacity to withstand hardships. Mindfulness plays a big role in ensuring that people have a smile on their faces instead of a frown.

Allows us to cry

We have become a people that are obsessed with projecting a tough image. Men are obsessed with coming off as stoic and women are trying very hard to look like men. Nobody wants to be perceived as weak. Interestingly, crying is commonly seen as something only weak people do. Due to this negative attitude toward crying, people are forced to suppress their bad emotions and these emotions usually build up into a cataclysmic explosion in the form of a mental breakdown. Mindfulness teaches us to perceive our bad emotions, experience them to the full, and then detach from them. Crying our hearts out is a fantastic way of ridding ourselves of bad emotions and give room to positivity and happiness. We should feel empowered, not weakened, by crying.

No more wasting time

Wasting your time is akin to throwing your life away. There are very many activities that we are involved in that don't immediately seem like wastage of time. But when we pay close attention to these things, we find out that they are indeed a time-drain. Mindfulness empowers us to curate our lives in such a manner that our time is used for meaningful pursuits. Mindfulness allows us to notice and get rid of the activities that don't matter in the big scheme of things. Thus, we have more time to pursue our goals and become fulfilled.

## Sleep quality

It's no secret that sleep plays a huge role in our levels of happiness. We could have the most money, live in the best house, and have the job we had always dreamed of since our early childhood, but if we lack enough sleep, we will never know true happiness. Sleep is vital because it helps us enter into a relaxed state of being and also replenishes our minds, thus we are able to face our reality from a point of mental stability.

## Chapter 9: Mindful Mistakes

Mindfulness or the ability to focus your mind on what you are currently doing without judgment. It involves giving full attention, being aware of different sensations and savoring life as it unfolds. Mindfulness practice has become a popular panacea against stress and other health issues like eating disorders, anxiety attacks, gastrointestinal problems as well as sleeplessness. However, people still do not completely understand what mindfulness is all about. There are myths that keep them away from trying this beneficial technique.

To help you better comprehend mindfulness and appreciate the benefits that it brings, here are some common "misconceptions" you need to be aware of:

Mindfulness is a magic cure

It is not. Mindfulness does not take away your pains or stress in just one day. It involves commitment, self-discipline, and repetitive action to master the technique. Repetition is the key to becoming the person who knows how to live mindfully. It is not about avoiding unpleasant sensations or feelings instead being aware, accepting and allowing them to pass. Mindfulness helps you experience various sensations, thoughts, and emotions without dwelling on them. With regular practice, being patient and trusting the process, you will soon be experiencing a more fulfilling life.

## Mindfulness is a quick fix technique

People want an instant remedy to fix the wrongs in their own lives. They expect mindfulness as one of quick fix techniques. Mindfulness is not an antidote to solve your stress, depression or anxiety. It is learning the fact that present time is the best moment to live your life. You may have previous experiences related to what you are doing right now but you are not allowing them to affect the new sensations you are experiencing. You may fear about the future outcome but you do not let the thought keeps you from giving your best now. You take charge of your life by savoring the present condition. You do not edit nor challenge accompanying experiences. You just live each moment purposely. You allow yourself to be you.

Mindfulness is the same as positive thinking

They are poles apart. Positive thinking is controlling your mind to focus on the silver linings and good things only to attract positive manifestations.

Mindfulness is allowing positive and negative thoughts, feeling or sensations to happen without attaching yourself to them.

Mindfulness is focusing on good thoughts

Mindfulness allows both positive and negative sensations to flow. It does not prevent negative thoughts like fear, doubts, and anxiety to happen. Practicing mindfulness helps you let them come into your mind but you do not acknowledge them or let them stay long. You believe that your present action is essential to produce positive results. You stay focused on what are doing. For instance, while drinking coffee, you think about the negative effect of caffeine but instead of going deeper on the matter, you pay more attention to the smell of its aroma, its distinct taste and the sensations you while drinking your hot cup of this beverage.

Mindfulness requires Lotus or meditation pose

Not necessarily. Mindfulness can be practiced while doing your everyday chores, sitting, walking or working. You do not need to be still or go to a quiet place. It can be done while you are in work mode, active mode or traveling mode. You are free to practice it anytime, anywhere in any position or circumstance.

Mindfulness is about keeping your mind busy thinking or understand

Your mind has a tendency to overthink. If you allow it to analyze, comprehend, dissect and go through details, you will be experiencing mental fatigue or loss of motivation to complete your task at hand. Mindfulness helps you realize that there are things that are meant to be experienced and enjoyed without the need to understand them. Allow yourself the freedom to relish every circumstance that comes into your life. Don't stress yourself thinking about its negative impact. Focus on what you need to do right now and complete it.

Stop yourself from overthinking about everything. This will keep you from enjoying the present moment. You only pass through life once, why to allow your present slips away by thinking about your past or future. Change the patterns of your thoughts and stop yourself from making sense of every situation that occurs because it will rob your chance to be happy. Stop being imprisoned with your thoughts. Start living in the realness of present time. It brings more happiness and peace of mind.

Mindfulness is about disregarding your past or future

Mindfulness allows you to appreciate past lessons, use them to avoid similar mistakes but you need to just keep them as history. Your present action matters because you are building your future. The outcome of your present choice and decisions significantly affect your future life. You know that your future is determined by how you choose to live your life now. When fears of the unknown come into your mind, you do not let them dampen your productivity level. You keep on doing your task and aim for its success. You understand that you are taking care of your future by creating quality output at the moment.

Mindfulness is being strict on yourself so you will become better

You can be better by being kind, loving, gentle and compassionate to yourself. Stop the habit of chastising yourself for who you were before. You may have done lots of mistakes and encountered failures in the past but living with regrets will keep you from enjoying present opportunities to be happy. Allow yourself the freedom to write your own story, re-edit it according to your new perspective and act on your wiser choice. Be mindful and aware of what is happening around you. Smell the flowers, inhale deeply, bask in the warmth of the sun, enjoy a small chat with friends and do everything with the purpose of having a meaningful connection. Feel, hear, smell, touch, taste and embrace every experience with a fresh attitude every day.

When you are aware of these misconceptions about mindfulness, you will be inspired to practice it. It gives heaps of benefits but above all, mindfulness helps you understand your great capacity to manage your own life.

## Chapter 10: Who And How Can Practice Mindfulness?

The first recipe for happiness is: avoid too lengthy meditation on the past.

- Andre Maurois

Who can practice Mindfulness?

This may seem to be a silly question for many, but it relates directly to the approach and scope of the Mindfulness practices in a precise manner. Anyone can practice these techniques without hesitation but you must seek expert guidance before beginning into it as well as have same primary readings beforehand. This helps in achieving your goals in faster manner.

## How can practice Mindfulness?

### Preparing You

As such there are no specific criteria or restrictions that abstain you from practicing the Mindfulness concepts. It is advisable to go through some of the books to understand the ideology of the concept and its implementations. This helps you in preparing for beginning into Mindfulness meditation.

### Basics of Mindfulness

As we all know it is required to understand the basics of any concept before practicing or beginning it. The same applies on Mindfulness meditation techniques. It is quite essential for you to understand about mindfulness, it's origin, implementations, benefits, misconceptions, possible drawbacks and more before you start into this field.

Adopting the basics

Once you are sure about practicing the Mindfulness practices it becomes equally important that you understand the basics about Mindfulness and its implantations so you may categorize yourself in rightful manner that helps you in tapping maximum benefits from your efforts.

Step by Step Approach

This is an important factor that may affect your plans and it is advisable that you begin under the guidance of an expert to understand systematic step-by-step methodology to practice mindfulness techniques. This can be best achieved if you seek expert guidance from a practitioner or coach who may help you in preparing custom plans for you.

Lifestyle Adaptation based approach

It is a critical factor for taking the right path while choosing appropriate techniques that suits you best. The beauty of mindfulness is that it can be easily adopted into your routine with minimal changes or additions once you learn the basic fundamentals about Mindfulness techniques and meditation practices.

Dedicated Beginners Approach

This may seem to be easy; but it required patience and dedicated efforts to achieve the desired results from Mindfulness techniques. The results may vary depending on your requirements and learning curve. The usual practices show that once can easily get command over the basic practices in about three weeks.

Custom Planning

As Mindfulness Techniques are devised to fulfill the requirements in different environment and subject it is quite required for a beginner to prepare the custom plan for achieving the desired results. This is extremely useful in resolving the various issues related the obsessive-compulsive disorders and anxiety related issues.

Mindfulness: The new dimension of the meditative approach

Whenever I feel blue, I start breathing again.

- L. Frank Baum

There are enormous definitions of meditation that can be understood in light of various civilizations, culture and healing practices. These contexts range from the ancient to modern developments and have substantial growth in various areas. The evolvement of Mindfulness can be also considered as the new dimension of the meditative approach that is used for psychiatric therapeutic applications.

Meditation in focus of mindfulness approach

The development in Meditations and related practices are beyond the scope of this book and in this chapter we will try to understand meditation in focus of mindfulness approach.

Meditation as an art

There are various options that can be considered as different meditation practices and related to various culture and civilizations. It can be considered as an art of adopting the techniques in a subtle manner that your body and mind has least resistance and supports its effects. This the basic point that puts meditation as an art. The perceptions and the feeling that are developed by attaining the higher states in meditative techniques is quite imperative and has an abstract feel that cannot be shared with anyone or may be documented by any means. This puts meditation as an art for practicing therapies like mindfulness and others.

Meditation as a science

The studies carried out on the practitioners while practicing meditation techniques have found to be in the alpha state of mind. It is the state of mind between Trans and Sleep and accounts for enhanced brain activities. In this state brain is more receptive and can be instructed to carry out the tasks that seem to be impossible in real time situations. This state of mind is in light sleep that can be achieved while you are awake with the help of the meditation techniques. These studies are documented scientifically that suggests Meditation as science.

## Meditation Ancient & Modern Contexts

Meditation date backs to different ancient and modern contexts. The ancient Yoga practices have described different type of Dhyan and provide various references related to the mutative techniques. Apart the spiritual practices in Buddhist and Zen meditations are also indicating the usage of meditations related methods and practices in ancient times. There are ample evidences that confirm that Meditation was prevailing from ancient time. Along with this there are different modern context where meditation is used for psychiatric practices to rule out various complications. The usage of Mindfulness in MBSR Program is one example of the developments related to modern application of the Meditation Techniques.

Meditation & Mindfulness

As discussed earlier, the Mindfulness approach is using meditation techniques as one of the basic fundamentals. It is the building block for the position when one can start with different approaches of applying mindfulness concepts in their life. These are quite dependent on the needs and situations for your complications or the requirements and it is quite essential to understand that without proper guidance and choosing the appropriate mediation technique it is almost impossible to learn practicing mindfulness in its real form.

Practicing medications

There are enormous ways of practicing meditation and it can be easily selected from the various prevailing methods that are used for mindfulness applications. The most popular five forms of meditation are Primordial Sound Meditation, Mindfulness-Based Stress Reduction, Zen, Transcendental Meditation, and Kundalini Yoga that are widely accepted and practiced by majority of people. It is quite confusing when we call mindfulness as a meditation practice here because till now we have put both Mindfulness and Meditation as separate in this book.

There are specific reasons why we discussed both as separate and different entity. Onwards the usage of the term

Meditation and Mindfulness can be considered as one meditative approach based on Mindfulness concept to rule out several complications. Onwards, we will discuss the contexts in unified manner that supports meditation approach for practicing the mindfulness concept. The main ideology behind discussing all these issue are to clear the confusions from the beginners mind and help them ascertain their requirements and complications which is a crucial factor in adopting the most appropriate mindfulness application.

Meditating Your Way

This is again one of the distinguishing features that sets mindfulness based meditation apart from the others. It is the simplest approach that focuses on usage of minimal instructions and changes to acquire command on the methods for practicing mindfulness meditations. If you are a beginner and you got a chance to learn the mindfulness meditation from an expert there are possibilities that they will put you in your most comfortable zone where you just have to focus yourself on the basic set of practices and your meditation process will start. This is the beauty of mindfulness that it has simplified the meditation practices so one can practice as he finds it comfortable. You will find that mindfulness has minimal amount of generic instructions required for practicing the mindfulness meditations.

## Chapter 11: Getting Ready To Practice Mindfulness

Meditation that leads to mindfulness has been recommended by many experts to minimize Stress, Anxiety and Conflict and also any issues regarding your daily life.

To effectively deal with Stress and Anxiety, you will need to trigger the natural relaxation response of the body by putting mindfulness techniques into practice. They will help you relax and it can happen through processes such as meditation, deep breathing, yoga and rhythmic exercises. We can reduce everyday stress by fitting such activities in our daily life in order to improve our mood and also energy.

Mindfulness can be practiced anywhere at any time. If you are interrupted by a loud noise or other people then you can swap consciousness and be in and out of a mindfulness state and that's ok. You don't need much time to practice and to eventually reap the rewards from it. Just as you spend 4 or 5 minutes brushing your teeth (or at least you should) you can also start practicing the state of mindfulness in 4 or 5-minute activities. Once you start you will notice that your anxiety levels will start to reduce almost instantly.

Try to find a calm place if possible, where you can meditate comfortably without being disturbed. Make sure that the place isn't too dark or too light and similarly too cold or too hot and try to have no contact with the outside world while you are doing this. This is your time, your place, your well-being.

Try to avoid any place which is more likely to have a lot of distractions. Having said this, you don't necessarily have to be at home. You can be outdoors at the beach, in the garden, at the park or anywhere you feel you can do this and which makes you feel comfortable.

Decide on a suitable position you'd like to be in. Being in sync with your posture is part of mindfulness too. You might prefer to sit with your legs crossed (with one leg on the other if you want – lotus position), to stand still in front of a mirror, lie down on the grass, your bed or the floor or you can even walk.

Your hands may be faced up with the fingers either gently touching the thumb or relaxed resting on your knees or thighs or gently folded on your lap. Your stomach and lower back should be relaxed and your chest upright.

In terms of your feet, you can for example place them so that the soles are touching each other and toes pointing away from the body.

Gently tilt your head forward to open up your airways

For beginners, lying on your back will be easier.

Relax your lower back and stomach — try to pinch your back to the ground as difficult as it may sound — literally lie down stick your back to the ground for counts of 30 seconds then release (Do these repeats of sticking your back to the ground and releasing every 30 seconda to start with then repeat this exercise multilple times a day, every day as many times you can!!!!. (No excuse, If you have kids then so do I and It/s all about making it happpen.) Do this multiple times a day when you remember to even if it has to be in ther pantry, and I gurantaee you are off too an excellent start!!!

A subconscious mind cannot differentiate reality from imagination. Your subconscious state of mind will work upon the descriptions or images you build within yourself or your mind, regardless the fact whether the images reflect the existing reality or not, Homework: when you go to bed, right before you fall aleep, focus on what your passions are, what interests you the most etc...

Our thoughts or beliefs are actually creative forces, and the moment we realize them, we start designing our day to day lives with more clarity & defined purposes.

## Chapter 12: Learning To Breathe Correctly

People always argue when I say they need to learn to breathe, but there are so many benefits to this exercise. The exercise will help you to lower your blood pressure. It will also slow your heartbeat. It helps you to stay in control of your emotions, and that's important. The breathing that takes place during meditation is a very standard pattern, but the difference between that and everyday breathing is that you are totally aware of it. That's the kind of breathing that we need to teach you. When you suffer from anxiety or panic, your breathing goes into overload, and you tend to hyperventilate. You must have seen people being asked to breathe into a paper bag. This is to help the levels of carbon dioxide to get back to normal within the body and is necessary for calmness.

Exercise in Mindful breathing

Students of mindfulness always go through breathing and relaxation techniques before tackling more advanced forms of mindfulness because these techniques are the foundation for mindfulness. If you can sit on a hard chair and place your feet flat on the floor, making sure that your back is completely straight and your head slightly bowed, this is the ideal position for the breathing exercise. You should be comfortable and in a place where you will get very little interruption. You should also be aware that tight clothing could affect the efficiency of your breathing.

Place your hands on your lap palms upward with your strongest hand supporting the other while your thumbs touch together. This helps you to become grounded so that you are not fiddling with your hands while doing the exercise. The reason we are doing this now is before you even consider doing any meditation, you need to learn to breathe correctly.

Breathe in through the nostrils to the count of seven and as you do so, concentrate on the energy entering your body. Imagine the airflow as being something solid and try to imagine the air going down into your body and lungs. Hold the breath for the count of four and then breathe out from either your nostrils or your mouth. The exhale isn't that important, so you can do this from your mouth. Breathing in through the nostrils is, however, crucial because when you always breathe in using this method, you are letting the air get filtered by the hairs in your nose, which means that it is purer.

Breathe in to the count of seven. Hold the breath for the count of three and then exhale to the count of eight. Keep doing this and notice that the upper abdomen part of the body should produce a pivoting motion as you do so. If you need to close your eyes to concentrate on your breathing, this may stop you from becoming distracted in the initial stages. If you find yourself thinking about anything other than the breathing, acknowledge the thought, let it go, and continue to think about the breathing.

This is an exercise that you can do once a day to help you to stay within the moment but also to get you into good habits with your breathing. People tend to slouch when they sit, and this stops the energy going into the right places. If you find that you do this, straighten your back. It is vital that the energy goes through your body when you breathe, and straightening of the spine will allow this to happen.

This is also the breathing method that you use with meditation, but we will go into that subject in a later chapter. For the time being, empty your mind. Be in the moment and breathe in, imagining the breath rushing into your body. Hold the air for the count given above and then breathe out. If you do this for about ten minutes in the morning and ten minutes at night, you help yourself to let go of stresses, and that's quite important. When you can do this, you will be able to use the breathing exercise when you find yourself in a stressed out situation to help you to gain your composure and get beyond the stress. Believe me; it does work.

Try to think of the body as having energy centers. These can be thought of in those simple terms, although in some religions are referred to as the chakras. If you are not breathing correctly or respecting your posture, you will find that these energy centers get blocked, and that's when troubles occur with health and with stress. Thus, your morning and evening session in calm breathing will help you to take control of your life in a much more fruitful way instead of letting your mind go off on a tangent, taking you into the realms of stress. This will make you into a happier person because you will be able to avoid letting yourself get stressed to the extent that it affects your body and the energy centers in your body.

## Chapter 13: Importance Of Staying Motivated

Enthusiasm is a key characteristic that we should have in life. That zest for life is important because it makes us keep working on what is entailed to us. Sometimes we find ourselves feeling like not doing anything. We may have a job, but every morning we find ourselves getting that feeling of not wanting to go to a job. This is a clear indication that we lack motivation. Motivation helps us stay determined and drives us to live a life we want. It's beneficial always to have motivation in life; we should not live a life with no motivation. Many factors make us lack motivation in life. You may be experiencing a difficult situation. Your job may not be paying well, and therefore you require the need to work. You may be stuck with debts and therefore lack the motivation to work hard in life because all your hard earned money ends up paying a debt. Change is what is needed to turn things around. You must maintain that desire to change so that the whole process will run smoothly.

One important thing about motivation is that it helps us accomplish our goals, it determines our success. So it is needed all through for us to be successful. Here is the importance of staying motivated.

You will be in the capacity to identify your goal.

A goal is set to achieve something in life. It may be a financial goal or a plan to change a behavior or an aspect of your life. What motivates you to set a target may be either positive or negative. You may not be happy with something in your life and be determined to change it. Also, you may be aspiring to have something that you don't have, and that can make you have a better life, all this will be as a attained through motivation. The motivation for improved circumstances inspires a goal, whether it is a yearning to add more, change or adding something new.

Action

We plan so many things but what makes those ideas come to reality? Motivation will make us turn our ideas into actions to attain that what we need in life. Planning is good, and it's even better to set our ideas into something tangible (accomplishment) to do so, we need constant and efficient actions and consistency in those action to attain goals. Why do some people fail to accomplish their plans while other does? Motivation is what determines whether we will achieve our goals or not. It is what keeps us going through ups and downs that are on our ways to reach our goals.

## Ability to Prioritize

Most of the time we have many goals to accomplish, and some are urgent while others may take some time. Time and energy are scarce resources, and therefore we need to share them accordingly.

Prioritizing our activities is one of the steps towards doing that. We need to work on the most important task first to achieve our best results. This happens as a result of motivation; it enables use to determine what or which activities should be prioritized.

Staying focused

Goals and tasks are not the same. Some are short term while others are a long time and will take a lot of time and resources to accomplish. What will make us stay focused on those goals that take lots of time to attain? It is easy to lose focus especially if the goals have not yet started bearing fruits; therefore, we need the motivation to help us stay focused on our goals. Motivation will help us keep taking consistency actions towards the accomplishment of your goals.

Overcoming a setback

Sometimes we are faced with a difficulty along the way, and we fail from time to time. Most of us tend to give up when they have failed for the first time. On the other hand, we see others fall and arise, some even fall so many times, but they still arise. What in particular makes those people rise again? Motivation ensures that we keep on going even after hitting an obstacle. Most of the goals that we need to achieve have obstacles on the way, and it is, therefore, important to pamper ourselves with motivation to keep on moving towards our goals.

As we have seen, there are many reasons for us to stay motivated. Life is all about having visions and setting goals. It also entails working towards achieving them and making our vision a reality. However, all this will just remain they way they are if we don't have the motivation to make them work. To stay motivated, you need to train yourself how to be motivated; you can start with something small such as imagining how you will be after accomplishing that goal. Then work towards achieving it no matter how small it is. Once you accomplish one to celebrate and start on another plan soon or later, you will find consistency motivation because you will be yearning to celebrate the achieved goal.

Ways to Helps You Stay Motivated

It is important always to stay motivated and as we have seen above staying motivated has much importance in our day to day life. Here are some ways that can help you stay motivated.

Keep reminding yourself about your goals – keeping track of your goal will help you stay focused on it and will help you review your progress to know how close or far you are from your goal.

Check your progress weekly – this will ensure that you stay on track and that you don't lose focus on your goal.

Celebrate every time you achieve your goal – rewards will make you want to accomplish another goal for you to celebrate.

Watch or read motivational speeches or stories — when you regularly read on what other people have achieved, you will begin to have a sense of motivation.

Get rid of your distractions — this should have come first; distractions will de-motivate you and will make you lose focus on your goals.

Split your goals into small attainable tasks — this will motivate you because that little work will seem simple to accomplish rather than the bigger goal.

Have a break — break will help you relax and enable you to have time to freshen up. You can visit places to rest simply; this will make you have a different environment from the usual one.

Mind your health – a healthy body will make sure that you perform to your very best, on the contrary, having an unfit body will de-motivate us, and this will make us perform poorly in what we do. No doubt that motivational is a part of our day to day life. It is, therefore, important to use this tips for use to stay motivated to get things going.

## Chapter 14: Techniques To Cultivate Mindfulness

It is actually quite easy to cultivate mindfulness. Mindfulness it nothing but "living your life as if it really mattered, moment by moment, by moment, as Job Kabat Zinn puts it. Here are some tips that you can focus on during your daily practice:

Focus entirely on breathing. When your emotions are intense, focus harder.

Pay attention to, all the sights, sounds and smells that you are surrounded by in a certain moment. They will just go unnoticed unless you consciously make an effort in the beginning. When you are at a higher level of awareness, this will become a habit.

The emotions and thoughts that creep in do not define the person you are. Keep this in mind. This simple insight will liberate you from your negative thoughts.

Tune in to all the physical sensations around you. Become aware of simple things like the temperature of the coffee when it meets you lips and how it feels in your mouth. When you eat food notice all the textures and tastes. This is a form of conditioning for your mind to be more aware.

There are certain techniques and exercises that can condition you to achieve a higher state of mindfulness. Here are some techniques that have been recommended by most practitioners of mindfulness meditation.

Scanning your body: Pay complete attention to your entire body. Start from the head and work this focus up to your toes or vice versa. This exercise allows you to experience everything that you sense. Try not to change any feeling that your experience during this exercise.

The raisin technique: Carefully observe a raisin using your senses slowly, one at a time. Think about the texture of the raising against your skin when you place it on your palm. This exercise may be practised with various foods. All you need to do is focus entirely on the moment you are in. The raisin is only a physical medium that makes this exercise easier. This is a great method for beginners. This conditions the mind and improves stamina until one can achieve this state of awareness on his own.

Walking meditation: This is great method to increase your awareness about the dynamics of your body. Walk around in a peaceful space. Pay close attention to every minute movement as your walk. Think about how your feet feel as they brush against the ground, the movement of your hips etc. Walking is a routine activity that we hardly pay any attention to. Since we do it always, we take it for granted. Try to practice this for about ten paces. Changing the walking surface helps you identify new experiences and feelings.

Love Kindness Meditation: This technique requires you to extend your compassion to people around you. Begin with a person you are close to. This could be your spouse or your child. Thereafter try to extend love, kindness and compassion to someone you know briefly. Lastly, you can even move on to a person who has been unkind to you at some point. Be mindful of the compassion that you are showing to the person. Since you are aware of the fact that you have some history or baggage with a certain person, not allowing those thoughts to interfere with your compassion is a great way to strengthen your mind.

These techniques of mindfulness meditation are extremely simple to follow.

It takes some practice to make them a habit so that you don't really have to think too much about a certain activity or a technique when you are including it in your daily routine.

## Chapter 15: Mindful Exercises 45 Minutes To An Hour

3 Mindfulness Exercise to do on a daily basis

Exercise 1: Mindful Immersion

This is a wonderful exercise that allows you to be content in the present and free yourself of getting caught up in daily routines. This will allow you to appreciate and notice the world as it evolves around you. Time us constantly moving. Many of us do not notice it moving by us. Do not let the world rush by. When you get caught up in wanting to simple finish a task, you do not appreciate the nature of the task. You do not notice the task. You simply do that and move on to the next and the next. There will always be a next task.

Whatever task you are doing, whether it is something you do once in while like repainting your room or an activity you do daily such as washing the dishes, you need to immerse yourself into the task and really experience it.

Let us take the example of house cleaning

1. Rather than do your chore like you always do, focus on all the details of the task. Open yourself up to a whole new world of new experiences. This is a wonderful new world of looking at every task. You should be able to feel and notice every motion of your arm and hands as you wash the dishes or sweep / vacuum the floor. Feel your muscles contracting and relaxing. Feel your fingers move and your hands too. When you scrub down the plates feel your hands move in perfect sync.

2. Notice the patterns that develop. The patterns you use for the task at hand. How the patterns repeat themselves as you do the action over and over. You can develop

better ways of doing the task. You can think of a different pattern to clean the window, or wash the dishes, or paint your room.

3. Try to focus solely at the task at hands, and really feel every sensation associated with the task at hands. As you do so, every day you will discover new experiences and rediscover those experiences every time you perform these seemly routine tasks.

You do not need to labor through your daily task only focus on finishing the task. You should become aware of every step of the task as you fully immerse yourself in task that you are performing. As you become immersed in the task open up all your senses and focus them on the task. How do the tasks make your feel? What are the sensations that go through you as you do this task?

As you do these routine task, clear your mind if all judgments and preconceptions. Every single task can be a physical, mental and spiritual exercise. This is what mindfulness entails.

Exercise 2: Mindful Listening

We are now moving on to another very pleasant ard deep reaching meditative exercise. One that involves one of your most emotional senses, your ear. We know the power of sounds. When we listen to music it can reach deep down into our souls and pour out emotions. We have to call upon this sense as we practice mindfulness. This mindfulness exercise allows and encourages you to open up your ears and listen to all the sounds around us without placing judgment.

At every point in time there are so many sounds around us, many of which we fail to hear because we are in a rush and **our minds are full**. So much of the way we perceive the world is based on past sounds we hear and the experiences these sounds are connected to. They can be bad experiences or good experiences. Mindful listening allows to listen to the sounds around us without placing any judge of them. Learn to listen to sounds without any preconceptions. Be neutral and in the moment.

1. Choose a song or music or maybe a classical composition or a musical score of a movie you have never heard or seen before. You can even choose the classical radio station or a station with a genre of music you do not usually listen to. Now wait until a music piece you have never heard before, or play the musical piece you have never heard before.

2. Put your headphones on and cut of your sense of sight by closing your eyes. Try to not judge the music by genre or title or musician. Try not to think about whether you like the music piece or not. Just allow

the sounds of the sounds to flow in and out of you. Think about the song and get lost in that music. Make sure your mind does not wonder off. Don't start thinking about your day or what you did or the tasks you have ahead. No! Just listen to that song and that song alone. Listen to every single element of that song. Notice every individual sound of the music piece. Explore the sounds.

Even if the song is one you don't like do not hate it. Allow your sense of hearing to be the only thing at work. Be aware of the music and be one with the sound waves.

3. You are to simply listen to the song and become entwined with all the elements and individual sounds of the song void of judgement, prejudice and preconception

of the type of music, the instruments used and even the lyrics.

Exercise 3: Mindful Appreciation

In the final exercise on this chapter we focus on an exercise that allows you to reflect upon your day and appreciate it.

Every day is to be appreciated. And if you go a day without appreciating, you are missing out on your day fully.

Take notice of just 7 things you did in the day. These should be activities that generally go unacknowledged. These things can be anything - tasks performed, objects or people. You have to decide. With your book and pencil / pen write down these 7 things at the end of your day.

So what is the point of mindful Appreciation? This exercise is to allow you to acknowledge and be grateful of all the supposing small occurrences in existence in life. All of these small things add value to our existence and all of them come together to make the world we see, and which if them have a purpose. But we fail to see this as we rush through life. Now that you are a mindful individual, you can now appreciate these things.

For example, you can appreciate the electricity that flows through our brains, hearts and all the electric devices you use, the mail man that delivers your packages and letters, the cat that visits your window ledge every day, the warmth of your sheets as you sleep in them, your nose that you use to smell the pleasant aromas of the world, your finger tips that allows you to feel even the smallest grain of salt, and so many more.

Think about how these thinks come in existence, how they actually work and how they are made.

Try to appreciate the benefits of having these objects in your life and the lives of all the people you know and love. Just acknowledge these objects

Think about a live without these objects. Will life even exist? Without electricity, our brains cannot communicate with our body. Our hearts will not beat. All our electric devices will not work. Appreciate all of these things we do not even notice.

Notice all the details of these objects. Even the smallest details. Have you noticed every single line in the prints of your finger tip? Have you appreciated all of these tiny details that makes you feel a tiny grain of salt as you rub it between your fingers?

Think about how all the things you listed at the end of the day are connected to you and you to them. How their functions impact your life and the world as a whole, and even the universe.

Find out as much as you can about all of these things: their creation, their purpose and their workings. You will learn to appreciate life instead of running through it.

## Chapter 16: Mindful Body: Creating The Body You Want With New Choices

How does your body feel and how do you feel about your body? You have been disconnected from your body all your life. Now is the time to establish that strong connection and get the best from your body. If you do not understand, your body's needs strongly enough to know what it wants at all times and how best to care for it, there will be a limit to what your body can help you achieve daily. It is time to break all those late night routines that stop you from giving your body the adequate sleep or night rests it deserves. Let us learn how to become more mindful of your body:

How to Become More Mindful of Your Body

Here are some ways you can become more mindful of your body and care for it more:

Pay more attention to what you eat

If you do not feel good about your body or your body does not feel right, maybe you have been eating the wrong kind of foods for far too long. It is time to do some mindful eating.

Before you take a bite of anything, stop and think about how it can affect your body and health. Will it make you fat? Will it increase your sugar levels? How much carbs and sugar is in it.

You need to start checking all the things you have been ignoring about the foods you eat, especially the processed and packaged foods. Check the sugar and calorie content before they find their way to your mouth.

Do you feel energized enough or are you fatigued?

You need to become more mindful of your sleeping habits and routines. Are you getting enough sleep at night? Are there things you do that rob you of your beautiful night rest? Ask yourself these questions and use the answers to make important lifestyle changes. Get rid of all late night activities such as watching TV shows late into the night, eating heavy foods that may cause discomfort while you are asleep, etc.

## Engage in 10 minutes of deep breathing before bedtime

A ten minutes deep breathing exercise will help you sleep better, help your muscles relax, and calm down your nerves. Simply lie as if you are ready to doze off, keep your eyes shut, draw in very long breaths, and exhale slowly. Keep one hand on your belly and one on your chest. Notice how the hand on your belly moves with each inhalation and exhalation. Focus on different muscles in your body and imagine them relaxing. You can begin from your legs and work your way to your crown or begin from your crown and go downwards.

Do more mindful physical workouts

You need to keep your body fit to ensure it keeps serving you without fail. Find time to exercise your muscles. If your body does not feel right, you can make it feel right by shedding some extra pounds through daily physical workouts. Enroll in a gym if you must or just set daily workout goals with your spouse.

You can run, jog, cycle, dance, swim, etc. While at it, pay attention to how your body feels before and after each workout session. Take note of the increased activity in your muscles, heart, and other areas. With time, you will start feeling a new surge of energy and become enthusiastic to do more.

## Mindful Relationships: How a New Point of View Can Dramatically Increase Your Happiness

Most relationships fail because of the imbalance created by our selfishness. We focus so much on what we want that we pay no attention to what the other person wants. We forget that the way to finding lasting happiness in any relationship is to make the other person happy.

Happiness in a relationship comes as a reward for making someone else or other people happy. Probably you have not been paying enough attention to the good sides of that person or commend them when they get things right. May be all you do is criticize or condemn him or her when he or she does not meet your expectations.

Take time to think about your closest and most cherished relationships. Create a list of all the things you are grateful for in your partner. These could be your partner's major strengths or the things he or she has done to help you become a better you, live a better life, or achieve your dreams. Here is what you can do:

Tell your partner how grateful you are for all he/she does for you

Once you have identified all the ways the important people in your life make your life more beautiful, tell them how grateful you are for having them in your life and appreciate every sacrifice they make to see you happy and successful.

Show them how grateful you are

Sometimes words alone may not be enough to show your gratitude. You may need to take a step or two further by buying them a special gift, taking them somewhere special and giving them a special treat or giving them a special treat at home by giving them a mindful sensual massage, cooking their favorite meal, etc.

Help them become better

Apart from making the person or people you care about happy, mindfulness helps you discover the areas they are lagging behind and where they could use your help to improve. Support their dreams and aspirations in whatever way you can. If they are working on a difficult project, you can lend a hand or help them find the right professional help when they need one desperately.

They will no doubt have their own bad sides and bad habits they are struggling with. Just like you made a list of the things you love and appreciate about them, make another list of the things you find annoyingly irritating about them.

How to Use Mindfulness to Improve Your Relationships

Here is what you can do with this list to make your relationship better:

Look at every item on the list of things you hate about your partner or something he or she does that drives you nuts. Ask yourself why you find that particular habit irritating. Ask yourself if someone else would find the same thing irritating. It could be that the problem is how you react to issues and not with your partner. That thing you find irritating may be funny or eccentric to someone else.

Put yourself in your partner's shoes. Pay attention to what is going on in your partner's business, office, academics, know their health condition and how things are with the other people they care about like their parents or siblings. If you were to go through what they are going through at this moment, would you still be sweet and pleasant or more annoying and irritating than you find them?

Taking these steps will help you deal with your partner with honest acceptance instead of being judgmental or embracing the resignation approach. Honest acceptance helps foster happiness in relationships despite what flaws or shortcomings your partner may have.

## Conclusion

By now you will have practiced at least six mindfulness meditations, hopefully a few times a day or more. You are already developing a new habit, the mindfulness habit, and it's my sincere hope that you have already begun to experience some of the many benefits mindfulness can bring. You have a journal, where you have been noting your responses and reflections to the meditation; you will have begun to experiment with all sorts of mindfulness practices, both in a formal, planned setting and just as you go about your daily life. What does that feel like for you? What new joys or insights have you discovered? Welcome to the beginning of a new and wonderful journey. I'll leave you with my favorite definition of mindfulness once again. I have this pinned on my notice board, to remind me to live my life in the now, and to be mindful. That is, after all, the best that we can aim to do.

www.ingramcontent.com/pod-product-compliance
Lightning Source LLC
Chambersburg PA
CBHW072006070526
44583CB00015B/1354